The Jiu-Jitsu Kangaroo

Monkey Mount

© Copyright 2022 – All rights reserved.

The content contained within this book may not be reproduced in any form on or by electronic or mechanical means, including information storage and retrieval systems, without permission in writing from the publisher, except by a reviewer who may quote brief passages in a review.

First paperback edition August 2022.

A word to grown-ups from Monkey Mount

Monkey Mount is a team of creatives and Jiu-Jitsu practitioners with a common goal: *to inspire others*. This community was created by Brazilian Jiu-Jitsu and Judo Black Belt Yacinta Nguyen with the intent of inspiring her students to see the magic in the martial arts that have transformed her life.

Professor Yacinta Nguyen is among the elite Brazilian Jiu-Jitsu practitioners in Canada. She holds accolades from the most prestigious competitions around the world and is also featured on the *BJJ Heroes* website. Moreover, her passion and focus now is to bring together the wonderful talent in the community and leverage Brazilian Jiu-Jitsu as a means to:

- empower our children through *confidence building* and *resilience training*
- show young girls that *strong is beautiful*
- improve *mental health* in the community

We hope you enjoy this coloring book as much as we enjoyed creating it. If you did, please consider taking a moment out of your busy day to leave us a review, this is more helpful than you can imagine and will allow us to keep on creating more books for the community.

With Love,

The Monkey Mount Team

 JOIN OUR COMMUNITY ON SOCIAL MEDIA!

@MONKEYMOUNTBOOKS

At recess one day it's clear something's wrong.
There on the playground, not a laugh or a song.

No one swinging or sliding. No one playing at all.
No jump ropes, no scooters, no frisbees, no balls.

Then all of a sudden, **they see someone there.**
A hippo just standing with spiky green hair.

"Oh no not again." "Please say it's not so."
They hope it's not true, but they already know.

Henry B. Hippo, a bully in school.
Created a new, not so fun bully rule.

He wouldn't let anyone use the playground.
He scared them away if they came around.

One of those animals was Kyle Kangaroo.
And he just didn't know what he should do.

His friends and him thought, "Well that's just unfair."
But what could they do with Henry right there?

Kyle told his parents and they had a plan.
"You can do it honey, just believe that you can."

They went to a class, so exciting and new.
A Brazilian martial art, they call **Jiu-Jitsu**.

The class taught Kyle confidence, to hold his head high.
That he can do anything as long as he tries.

His teacher taught him rolling, that's sparring with others.
And he practiced at home with his father and mother.

Then in no time, he felt strong and he knew.
That school day at recess just what he should do.

Kyle's friends gathered 'round him, not sure what to think.
Then out ran old Henry, as quick as a wink.

Kyle stood on the playground right next to the swings.
"Hey Henry, can we talk about a few things?"

Henry just laughed saying, " And who are you?"
"I'm the one and the only Jiu-Jitsu Kangaroo."

"I want you to let everyone play here again.
We can all play together. We can all be good friends."

"Playing alone can't be any fun.
There's so much you can't do, when there's only one."

"No tag and no races. No kick ball or catch.
No chalk drawing contests or big dodge ball match."

Henry walked right up to him. **Looked him right in the eyes.**
Kyle stood his ground, to Henry's surprise.

Because of his training he felt strong, in control.
And confident that he would accomplish his goal.

Henry didn't quite know, just what to do next.
He was confused and befuddled and a little perplexed.

"No one has ever, stood up to me.
But now that you have, it's quite plain to see."

"My days hogging the playground are over and done.
And playing alone was not very much fun."

All the friends overheard this and started to cheer.
Lifting Jiu-Jitsu Kangaroo high in the air.

From that moment on Henry realized one thing.
It's not fun to rule the kingdom if you're alone as the king.

He stopped all his bullying and instead made a friend.
Jiu-Jitsu Kangaroo and that's not the end.

Kyle and Henry both practiced together.
Learning from each other, getting better and better.

Jiu-Jitsu helped both of them learn something new.
Henry and his friend **Jiu-Jitsu Kangaroo.**

The End

Made in United States
Troutdale, OR
04/04/2025